THE DECADENT POETRY
OF THE EIGHTEEN NINETIES

JOHN M. MUNRO

The
Decadent Poetry
of the
Eighteen-Nineties

1970
AMERICAN UNIVERSITY OF BEIRUT
Beirut, Lebanon

Library of Congress Catalog Card Number: 73 – 131229

© 1970 by the American University of Beirut. All rights reserved

Printed by the Heidelberg Press – Lebanon, Beirut

For those who reminded me that true scholars are also gentlemen

FOREWORD

WHAT FOLLOWS was originally intended as an introduction to a much larger work, a collection of essays by various scholars on the Decadent poets of the 1890's, followed by a representative selection of their verse. Unfortunately this ambitious project had to be abandoned when it became apparent that the size of such a volume would daunt even the most altruistic of publishers. An attempt was made to reduce the encyclopedic range of the original collection, but this also was unsatisfactory, and though it resulted in a study of commercially viable proportions, its usefulness was sorely diminished. A victim, perhaps, of *une folie de grandeur*, I was made to realise that the cause of Nineties scholarship might best be served by publishing the individual essays separately, and many of the original contributors have since withdrawn their essays and published them elsewhere.

During the long and debilitating illness and subsequent death of my once promising brainchild, the rest of the family remained faithfully in attendance, proferring advice, sympathy, and encouragement. Now the poor, misbegotten creature is dead, and it remains for me to thank those who devoted so much of their time and energy in the vain attempt to keep the patient alive. To Robert L. Peters of the University of California at Irvine, who not only provided valuable editorial assistance in helping me to assemble the original manuscript, but read an early draft of the present study as well, my thanks are especially due. Both he and Karl Beckson, who also read this essay at an earlier stage, saved me from occasional informational and stylistic embarassments and made a number of valuable suggestions. The responsibility for whatever errors that may remain, however, is of course my own.

I am also indebted to Ian Fletcher, R. Kelsey R. Thornton, J. Benjamin Townsend, Clyde de L. Ryals, R.D. Brown, Timothy d'Arch Smith, Ruth Z. Temple, David Carroll, Thomas Jay Garbaty, and many other specialists and scholars of the literature of the eighteen-nineties, which exigencies of space rather than lack of appreciation inhibit me from mentioning by name. All of them displayed considerable patience and tact during the frustrating period when it appeared that there was still hope that a full scale study of the Decadent poetry of the Nineties might be published. I am aware that I cannot ever hope to repay these people for their kindness and consideration, but in dedicating this slender volume to them, I wish to place on record a sincere acknowledgment of my indebtedness.

Finally, I wish to record my gratitude to Dr. William Bickers and the Publications Committee of the American University of Beirut, who made the publication of this study possible; to Zahi Khuri, who was responsible for its layout and design; and to George Taylor, who read both the final typescript and proofs.

Beirut, 1970

ILLUSTRATIONS

Walter Sickert's *Joe Haynes and Little Dot Hetherington at the Old Bedford Music Hall.*

W.P. Frith's *Derby Day.*

Sir John Everett Millais' *Bubbles.*

James Abbott McNeill Whistler's *Nocturne in Black and Gold.*

Dante Gabriel Rossetti's *Lady Lilith*

John Lane.

Cover design of *The Yellow Book.*

Cover design of Lord de Tabley's *Poems: Dramatic and Lyrical.*

Cover design and sample page from John Gray's *Silverpoints.*

Cover design of John Addington Symonds' *In the Key of Blue.*

Leonard Smithers.

Title page of Theodore Wratislaw's *Orchids.*

CONCERNING A MISUSED TERM:

viz. "Art" as recently applied to a certain form of literature.

Is this, then "Art"— ineffable conceit,
Plus worship of the Sadi-tainted phrase,
Of pseud-Hellenic decadence, effete,
Unvirile, of debased Petronian ways?

Is this your "Culture", to asphyxiate,
With upas-perfume sons of English race,
With manhood-blighting cant-of-art to prate,
The jargon of epicene disgrace?

Shall worse than pornographic stain degrade,
The name of "beauty," Heav'n imported dower?
Are *they* fit devotees, who late displayed,
The symbol of a vitriol-tainted flower?

And shall the sweet and kindly Muse be shamed
By unsexed "Poetry" that defiles your page?
Has Art a mission that may not be named,
With "scarlet sins" to enervate the age?

All honour to the rare and cleanly prints,
Which have not filled our homes from day to day
With garbage—epigrams and pois'nous hints
How asthete—hierophants fair Art betray!

If such be "Artists," then may Philistines
Arise, plain sturdy Britons as of yore,
And sweep them off and purge away the signs
That England e'er such noxious offspring bore.

Anon
(*Punch*, April 13, 1895).

I

THE IMPULSE to categorize has long been a besetting sin of literary historians, and though one can understand and to some extent condone the practice of grouping a number of writers behind a seemingly appropriate banner, it is obvious that such a habit frequently lends itself to over-simplification and distortion. Nowhere is this more clearly demonstrated than among the writers who made their reputations during that period loosely referred to as the eighteen-nineties.

If, for example, one considers only the poets who were writing during the last decade of the nineteenth century, it is clear that far from constituting a neat, relatively homogeneous unit about which one may generalize with some assurance, they exhibit such a variety of beliefs and attitudes, to say nothing of techniques, that the conscientious literary historian if he wishes to present a true image of the decade must abandon his impulse to categorize. Even if we dismiss Tennyson, Swinburne, Christina Rossetti, William Morris and Coventry Patmore, all of whom lived beyond the year 1890, on the grounds that they rightly belong to an older generation, what is one to make of such widely different poets as Oscar Wilde, William Watson, Arthur Symons, Thomas Hardy, Alfred Austin, George Russell (AE), A.E. Housman, Rudyard Kipling, Ernest Dowson, W.E. Henley, W.B. Yeats, Robert Bridges, John Davidson, Alice Meynell, Henry Newbolt, Lionel Johnson, Wilfred Scawen Blunt and Francis Thompson? Some of them subscribed to the more orthodox forms of religious belief, some were agnostics, and at least one was an atheist; some were intensely patriotic, others were not; some sang of the country, some of the town; some proclaimed the glories of their age, and others found little in contemporary life worth praising; some were cheerful, and some were melancholy; some were content to utilize traditional English forms, while others looked to France for their models, and Kipling was criticised for not writing poetry at all. Indeed, all that one can say of these poets as a whole is that they demonstrate the impossibility of attributing to them anything which could be regarded as a common unifying force.

Thus the word "decadent" when used in relation to the literature of the late nineteenth century should be used with caution. Nevertheless, like all catch-words, "decadent" has sufficient truth in it at least partially to justify its use in describing the character of the period, and though one should always remember that the Nineties probably produced as many aggressive, righteous, sober and God-fearing men as any other decade, there were also a fairly numerous group whose beliefs and attitudes seemed to run counter to what we have come to regard as typically Victorian.

However, even if we recognise two main streams in the literature of the Nineties, which for convenience we may call "Decadent" and "Counter-Decadent," there are still problems, for Oscar Wilde, Richard Le Gallienne, John Davidson, W. E. Henley and Robert Louis Stevenson all wrote poems which belong some in one group and some in the other, while Lionel Johnson, though usually included among the Decadents, also parodied them. Furthermore, the Rhymers' Club, that informal group of poets which began to meet in an upstairs room of the Cheshire Cheese in 1891, and included among its members such notable *fin-de-siècle* poets as Arthur Symons, Ernest Dowson and Richard Le Gallienne, was far from being the rallying point of the Decadent Movement, as is popularly supposed. Their two anthologies, *The Book of the Rhymers' Club* (1892) and *The Second Book of the Rhymers' Club* (1894), contained poetry which ranged from the most melancholy, introspective expressions of dispirited malaise to resounding, energetic exhortations to work for a better world.

Finally, to confuse the situation still more, there is the difficulty in determining what the word "decadent" means when applied to late nineteenth-century literature. Generally the word "decadent" was bandied about in the Nineties as a term of opprobrium or approval, by the self-appointed spokesmen for public morality on the one hand, and by the daring young sophisticates on the other. Occasionally, however, there was an attempt to take stock and discover what the term really meant. For example, in a review of Churton Collins' *Illustrations of Tennyson*, included in the first volume of Richard Le Gallienne's *Retrospective Reviews: A Literary Log* (1896), the writer drew a sharp distinction between decadence in style and decadence in literature. The former he took to be "Euphuism—and its antithesis, slang," while the latter was, as he put it, "the euphuistic expression of isolated observations," that is to say, "limited thinking, often insane thinking." In July 1894, in the second number of *The Yellow Book*, Max Beerbohm offered his definition of decadence, suggesting that it was characterized by "paradox and marivaudage, lassitude, a love of horror and all unusual things, a love of argot and archaism and the mysteries of style."

Perhaps the neatest description of the qualities of a decadent was provided by Lionel Johnson in an essay entitled "The Cultured Faun," which appeared in the *Anti-Jacobin*, March 1891:

Take a young man, who had brains as a boy, and teach

him to disbelieve everything that his elders believe in matters of thought, and to reject everything that seems true to himself in matters of sentiment. He need not be at all revolutionary; most clever youths for mere experience's sake will discard their natural or acquired convictions. He will then, since he is intelligent and bright, want something to replace his earlier notions. If Aristotle's *Poetics* are absurd, and Pope is no poet, and politics are vulgar, and Carlyle is played out, and Mr. Ruskin is tiresome, and so forth, according to the circumstances of the case, our youth will be bored to death by the nothingness of everything. You must supply him with the choicest delicacies, and feed him upon the finest rarities. And what so choice as a graceful affectation, or so fine as a surprising paradox? So you cast about for these two, and at once you see that many excellent affectations and paradoxes have had their day. A treasured melancholy of the German moonlight sort, a rapt enthusiasm in the Byronic style, a romantic eccentricity after the French fashion of 1830, a "frank, fierce," sensuousness à la jeunesse Swinburnienne; our youth might flourish them in the face of society all at once, without receiving a single invitation to private views or suppers of the elect. And, in truth, it requires positive genius for the absurd to discover a really promising affectation, a thoroughly fascinating paradox. But the last ten years have done it. And a remarkable achievement it is.

Externally, our hero should cultivate a reassuring sobriety of habit, with just a dash of the dandy. None of the wandering looks, the elaborate disorder, the sublime lunacy of his predecessor, the "apostle of culture." Externally, then, a precise appearance; internally, a catholic sympathy with all that exists, and "therefore" suffers, for art's sake. Now art, at present, is not a question of the senses so much as of the nerves. Botticelli, indeed, was very precious, but Baudelaire is very nervous. Gautier was adorably sensuous, but M. Verlaine is pathetically sensitive. That is the point: exquisite appreciation of pain, exquisite thrills of anguish, exquisite adoration of suffering. Here comes in a tender patronage of Catholicism: white tapers upon the high altar, an ascetic and beautiful young priest, the great gilt monstrance, the subtle-scented and mystical incense, the old-world accents of the Vulgate, of the Holy Offices; the splendour of the sacred vestments. We kneel at some hour, not too early for our convenience, repeating that solemn Latin, drinking in those Gregorian tones, with plenty of modern French sonnets in memory should the sermon be dull. But to join the Church! Ah, no! better to dally with the enchanting mysteries, to pass from our dreams of delirium to our dreams of sanctity with no coarse facts to jar upon us. And so these refined persons cherish a double "passion," the sentiment of repentant yearning and the sentiment of rebellious sin.

To play the part properly a flavor of cynicism is recommended: a scientific profession of materialist dogmas, coupled—for you should forswear constancy—with gloomy chatter about "The Will to Live." If you can say it in German, so much the better; a gross tongue, partially redeemed by Heine, but an infallible oracle of scepticism. Jumble all these "impressions" together, your sympathies and your sorrows, your devotion and your despair; carry them about with you in a state of fermentation, and finally conclude that life is loathsome yet that beauty is beatific. And beauty—ah, beauty is everything beautiful! Isn't that a trifle obvious, you say? That is the charm of it, it shows your perfect

5

simplicity, your chaste and catholic innocence. Innocence of course: beauty is always innocent, ultimately.
No doubt there are "monstrous" things, terrible pains,
the haggard eyes of the *absintheur*, the pallid faces of
"neurotic" sinners; but all that is the portion of our
Parisian friends, such and such a "group of artists,"
who meet at the Café So-and-So. We like people to
think that we are much the same, but it isn't true. We
are quite harmless, we only concoct strange and subtle
verses about it. And, anyway, beauty includes everything; there's another sweet saying for you from our
"impressionist" copybooks. Impressions! that is all.
Life is mean and vulgar, Members of Parliament are
odious, the critics are commercial pedants; we alone
know Beauty, and Art, and Sorrow, and Sin. Impressions
exquisite, dainty fantasies; fiery-coloured visions; and
impertinence struggling into epigram, for "the true,"
criticism; *c'est adorable!* And since we are scholars and
none of your penny-a-line Bohemians, we throw in
occasional doses of "Hellenism": by which we mean
the Ideal of the Cultured Faun. That is to say, a flowery
Paganism, such as no "Pagan" ever had: a mixture of
"beautiful woodland natures," and "the perfect come-
liness of the Parthenon frieze," together with the elegant
langors and favourite vices of (let us parade our "decadent" learning) the *Stratonis Epigrammata.* At this
time of day we need not dilate upon the equivocal charm
of everything Lesbian. And who shall assail us?—what
stupid and uncultured critic, what coarse and narrow
Philistine? We are the Elect of Beauty: saints and
sinners, devils and devotees, Athenians and Parisians,
Romans of the Empire and Italians of the Renaissance.
Fin de siècle! Literature is a thing of beauty, blood and
nerves...

In "The Cultured Faun" Johnson effectively enumerates those qualities typical of those poets whom we call Decadent; but it would be wrong to conclude that the English Decadence was no more than a rather unhealthy, ludicrous literary fad. Le Gallienne, Beerbohm and Johnson dismiss the movement with contempt, but to Arthur Symons literary decadence deserved sympathetic consideration, and in his important essay, "The Decadent Movement in Literature," published in *Harpers' New Monthly Magazine* (November 1893), he set out to justify this kind of writing, endeavoring to show that it was a serious literary movement not unlike that of the Greek and Latin Decadence. It is characterised, he wrote, "by an intense self-consciousness, a restless curiosity in research, an over-subtilising refinement upon refinement, a spiritual and moral perversity." And, he continued, "if what we call the classic is indeed the supreme art—those qualities of perfect simplicity, perfect sanity, perfect proportion, the supreme qualities—then this representative literature of today, interesting, beautiful, novel as it is, is really a new and beautiful and interesting disease." Nevertheless, such literature is typical of our civilisation, which has grown "over-luxurious, over-inquiring, too languid for the relief of action, too uncertain for any emphasis in opinion or conduct." It reflects all the moods and manners of a sophisticated society, and just as we lack "simplicity, sanity, proportion" in our lives, we should not expect to find them in our literature.

Apart from defining what the English Decadence was, there is, then, another problem in deciding whether it deserves to be taken seriously as a definite, if somewhat ill-defined, literary movement, or simply as an amusing interlude of no real literary or historical value. Neither problem admits of an easy solution. In general terms, however, we may say that the English Decadence, as defined by contemporaries, was concerned with the exploration of abnormal psychology; it professed to be concerned with Beauty, but with a beauty so bizarre and unconventional that one might feel more justified in calling it ugliness; it was self-conscious to the point of artificiality; it was generally at odds with the prevailing notions of decency and morality; it was somewhat precious and formal in style, sometimes betraying more concern with expression than subject matter; it was contemptuous of popular movements and attitudes; and it was imbued with a tone of lassitude and regret. Furthermore, it was asssociated with the young and was sometimes regarded as symptomatic of the age, but unlike the Imagist Movement of a decade or so later, it had no definite program and, apart from Symons in his *Harpers' Magazine* article, no real spokesman. For some it was an intensely serious affair, while for others, usually those who stood outside the movement, it was a rather distasteful exhibition of misguided intelligence. In short, it is only in the most general terms that we may speak of a "Decadent Movement." Even then we should be cautious of ascribing to it precisely determined characteristics.

II

SYMONS had drawn attention to the relationship between the literature and the age, and had stated that it was only natural to expect the one to mirror the other. Max Nordau, the most vehement antagonist of the Decadents, held precisely the same opinion, which he propounded at length in a pseudo-scientific treatise called *Degeneration* (1895), originally published in German under the title *Entartung*, in 1892, but soon translated into English and reprinted various times. In the civilized world, he wrote, "there obviously prevails a twilight mood," the main characteristics of which are "degeneration and hysteria," both evidently the consequence of "the excessive wear and tear suffered by the nations through the intense demands on their activity, and through the rank growth of large towns." Nordau further maintained that the writers of the age, for all that had been said to the contrary, offered no "ecstatic prophecy," but instead displayed "the senseless stammering and the babbling of deranged minds," and "what the ignorant hold to the outbursts of gushing, youthful vigour and turbulent constructive impulses are really nothing but the convulsions and spasms of exhaustion."

For Nordau, Europe was approaching its Armageddon; disaster was just around the corner. Looking back from an age threatened by wholesale atomic destruction, it seems curious that the closing years of Victoria's reign should have inspired such pessimism, for in contrast with our own time the eighteen-nineties seems to have been a period of positive action and hope. Throughout the century the populace had become increasingly better educated, more adequately housed and fed, in better health, and more prosperous. By the end of the century working conditions had everywhere improved, parliamentary reform had assured every man of his vote, and there were signs that intelligence and ability might some day become as necessary for advancement as good manners and upper class parents. Such scientific marvels as the automobile, electric lighting, moving pictures, the X-ray and the telephone were being invented, and machines which flew through the air or sailed under the sea were being talked about as practical realities, and, indeed, no miracle seemed beyond man's dreams or capabilities.

Nevertheless, as a result of this progress, the old order was threatened. The Industrial Revolution stimulated the growth of the middle class, further distorting the hierarchical structure of society which had been undergoing a gradual but inevitable revision since the later Middle Ages, and the working classes were at last becoming articulate and conscious of their corporate power. No longer did they feel inclined to tug forelocks and acknowledge that they knew their place. Instead, they went on strike for higher wages and improved working conditions, demonstrated in Hyde Park, and were increasingly active in politics. The family structure was changing too. The traditional Victorian household was presided over by a benevolent patriarch whose word was law and to whom everyone else deferred. Now women began to assert their freedom, campaigned for the right to vote, rode bicycles, and entered the professions. The influence of the Church was declining, partly because it had largely neglected the masses in the cities, partly because it had failed to come to terms with the scientific discoveries of such people as Lyell and Darwin, and no longer did the eternal verities seem quite so timeless or so true. Finally, as the century drew to a close, the Boer War added to the excitement and uncertainty.

Thus, in spite of manifest signs of progress, it was understandable that many should have felt that their age was in decline. Furthermore, even though one can demonstrate that throughout the nineteenth century the material well-being of the populace had improved, it is equally clear that material progress had brought with it a decline in spiritual values. As D. H. Lawrence put it some years later in an essay called "Nottingham and the Mining Countryside," first published in the *Adelphi* in 1930:

The great crime which the moneyed classes and promoters of industry committed in the palmy Victorian days was the condemning of the workers to ugliness, ugliness, ugliness: meanness and formless ugly surroundings, ugly ideals, ugly religion, ugly hope, ugly clothes, ugly furniture, ugly houses, ugly relationships between workers and employers.

Of course Lawrence was rather unfair in putting the blame squarely on the shoulders of "the moneyed classes and promoters of industry," just as he was unnecessarily restrictive in maintaining that it was only the working class which was condemned to "ugliness." But in recognizing the failure to observe aesthetic values which should accompany the march of material progress, he echoed one of the most frequently voiced criticisms of the age.

It is against this background of change and uncertainty, material prosperity and spiritual poverty, that the poetry of the English Decadence must be viewed. Revolt and the deliberate flaunting of convention were in the air, and it became almost axiomatic to undermine the cherished beliefs and attitudes of the solid, more conservative, outwardly respectable members of society. At the same time, however, there was a genuine concern about the "ugliness" of the age, and many writers at the end of the century made valiant attempts to restore some of the daily beauty which they felt had been lost from their lives. Previously, Carlyle, Ruskin, Tennyson and Matthew Arnold had all noted the decline of spiritual values; but their primary concern was to mold the existing pattern rather than to destroy it. The Decadents, on the other hand—or at least some of them—seem to have favored the latter, believing that the most effective way this could be accomplished was by inverting those values which the thrifty, industrious God-fearing upholders of Podsnappery held sacred. So it was that the Decadents—some with more genuine faith than others—maintained that aesthetic values were the only ones worth preserving, and that they ought to be safeguarded at all costs, even at the expense of sacrificing one's health or moral well-being. "What care I that the virtue

11

of some sixteen-year-old maiden was the price paid for Ingres' *La Source,*" cried George Moore in *Confessions of a Young Man* (1888). "That I should have *La Source,* that exquisite dream of innocence, to think of till my soul is sick with delight of the painter's holy vision.... Oh, for excess, for crime! I would give many lives to save one sonnet by Baudelaire!"

In short, the Decadents believed that it was art, not life, that really mattered, and if one could perpetuate this doctrine and at the same time upset the equilibrium of the middle class, so much the better. Thus, towards the end of the century there grew a tendency among many of the young writers of the time to exalt the unconventional, the morbid, the exotic, and the perverse. Virtue was disregarded in favor of vice, and sin was held to be an agent of transcendence. "What is termed sin," wrote Oscar Wilde in *Intentions* (1891), "is an essential element of progress. Without it the world would stagnate, or grow old or become colourless. By its curiosity, sin increases the experience of the race. Through its intensified asssertion of individualism, it saves us from the monotony of type. In its rejection of the current notions about morality, it is one of the higher ethics." And so Dorian Gray, the hero of Wilde's sensational novel of the same name, "looked on evil simply as a mode through which he could realise his conception of the beautiful."

In a sense, then, the Decadent literature of the Nineties was a rejection of established values. Partly it was a conscious inversion of the way of life associated with the respectable middle class; partly it was an attempt to affirm the importance of beauty and art. Thus the contemporary enthusiasm for the artificial was born out of a desire to shock, but also out of a wish to find beauty in what the average person considered commonplace or ugly. So when Arthur Symons felt called upon to justify his choice of subject matter in his collection of poems, *Silhouettes,* he asked in the preface to the second edition of that work in 1896:

> Is there any 'reason in nature' why we should write exclusively about the natural blush, if the delicately acquired blush of rouge has any attraction for us? Both exist: both, I think, are charming in their way: and the latter, as a subject, has, at all events, more novelty. If you prefer your 'new mown hay' in the hayfield, and I, it may be, in a scent bottle, why may not my indivudal caprice be allowed to find expression as well as yours? Probably I enjoy quite other scents and sensations as well, and I take the former for granted, and write my poem, for a change, about the latter. There is no necessary difference in artistic value between a good poem about a flower in the hedge and a good poem about the scent in a sachet. I am always charmed to read beautiful poems about nature in the country. Only, personally, I prefer town to country; and in the town we have to find for ourselves, as best we may, the *décor* which is the town equivalent of the great natural *décor* of field and hills. Here it is that artificiality comes in: and if anyone sees no beauty in the effects of artificial light in all the variable, most human, and yet most factitious town landscape, I can only pity him, and go on my way.

True to his aesthetic principles Symons, as well as others among his Decadent contemporaries, found the music hall artistically stimulating. Here was a place where the artificial and the *risqué* combined to provide an irresistible appeal. It inspired several paintings by the British Impressionist Walter Sickert, and a number of poems by Symons and John Davidson and also by Theodore Wratislaw, one of Symons' more ardent disciples, who was the author of "At the Empire," included in his collection *Orchids* (1896):

13

The low and soft luxurious promenade,
Electric-light, pile carpet, the device
Of gilded mirrors that repeat you thrice;
The crowd that lounges, strolls from yard to yard;

The calm and brilliant Circes who retard
Your passage with the skirts and rouge that spice
The changeless programme of insipid vice,
And stun you with a languid strange regard;

Ah! what are these, the perfume and the glow,
The ballet that coruscates down below,
The glittering songstress and the comic stars,

Ah! what are these, although we sit withdrawn
Above our sparkling tumblers and cigars,
To us so like to perish with a yawn?

The painter, Whistler, also sought beauty in the artificial, and in a passage in his *Ten O'Clock Lecture* (1890) he too suggested that for those who had eyes to see it, the town had a beauty of its own which compared favorably with the more conventional picturesqueness of the countryside:

And when the evening mist clothes the riverside with poetry, as with a veil, and the poor buildings lose themselves in the dim sky, and the tall chimneys become campanili, and the warehouses are palaces in the night, and the whole city hangs in the heavens, and fairyland is before us—then the wayfarer hastens home; the working man and the cultured one, the wise man and the one of pleasure, cease to understand as they have ceased to see, and Nature, who for once has sung in tune, sings her exquisite song to the artist alone, her son and her master—her son in that he loves her, her master in that he knows her.

To an age brought up to admire the sentimental prettiness of Millais' *Bubbles* and the documentary realism of W.P. Frith's *Derby Day*, Whistler's paintings came as a shock. The Victorian art critic and aesthetician John Ruskin, for one, was horrified, and referred to Whistler's *Nocture in Black and Gold* as a "pot of paint" flung in the public's face, a criticism curiously inconsistent with his earlier defense of Turner, a painter in some ways similar to the one he now attacked. For Ruskin, however, it was not simply Whistler's choice of subject matter which gave offense, but also his conception of what it meant to be an artist. Ruskin maintained that the artist and the artifact were inextricably involved, and what the artist created was conditioned by his personality and the ethical climate of his age. Whistler, on the other hand, believed that it was the business of the artist merely to select and arrange colors and forms to create a harmonious design, and the effectiveness of his work depended solely on his genius in arranging the proper materials in the proper way. As he stated it in *The Ten O'Clock Lecture:* "Art should be independent of clap-trap, should stand alone, and appeal to the artistic sense of eye and ear, without confounding this with emotions entirely foreign to it, as devotion, pity, love, patriotism and the like."

To such a doctrine many of the Decadent poets subscribed, and just as Whistler's paintings provoked in certain quarters violent opposition, so the poetry of the Decadents aroused considerable antagonism too. The Victorians liked their art to be refulgent with what Whistler called "clap-trap," and when it wasn't they were disappointed. And when they were asked to admire an artistic arrangement of commonplace, even sordid, components, they were very angry indeed. Yet outrageous though such art may have appeared to many in the Nineties, with the benefit of hindsight we can discern the inevitable progress to the Decadents' position.

15

III

IN *Culture and Anarchy* (1896), Matthew Arnold had been heavily satiric at the expense of the "philistines." Yet, in stressing the educational function of literature, Arnold subscribed to essentially the same view as those he attacked. It is true that he was sophisticated enough to substitute the classics for the sentimental moralizing of Mrs. Hemans and the proverbial philosophy of Martin Tupper, emphasizing that great literature should refine the sensibilities rather than provide direct examples of virtuous conduct. Yet, in consistently maintaining the necessity of great literature to be morally instructive, his approach was conservative. What is more, Arnold had little time for poets of what he called "the Keatsian kind," poets who, he said, "hovered over the tumult of life but who never really put their hand to it." Nevertheless, in insisting that literature could provide a guide to conduct without necessarily making a direct didactic assault, he did open the way for others who would insist that any art with pretensions to beauty—painting, sculpture, music, or indeed anything else—could assert a similar kind of influence. So it was that Walter Pater was able to preach his own gospel of aestheticism, widening the scope of Arnold's theory to take in all the arts, and shifting the emphasis from Arnold's stoical self-restraint to an impassioned Epicureanism, which glorified the senses and asserted the value of a "certain kind of temperament, the power of being moved by the presence of beautiful objects."

Pater was responsible for popularizing the cult of art for art's sake in England. He did not invent the term, nor was he the first to put forward the kind of aesthetic it properly implies. Actually the idea of art for art's sake has a fairly long and respectable history, going back at least as far as

16

the German Transcendentalists, notably Kant, whose theory that a work of art has "purposiveness without purpose" has been taken by Rose Frances Eagan, the leading authority on the subject, as the germ of the later idea. As Professor Eagan has said, the phrase should properly be applied to the doctrine which insists that the artistic product creates its own standards and terms of reference, and therefore should not be criticized on such extraneous grounds as conventional morality or widely accepted notions of what is appropriate to a particular genre, subject or occasion. This is what Gautier understood by art for art's sake when in the Preface to *Albertus* (1832) he stated: "La peinture, la sculpture, la musique, ne servent absolument à rien," and added, "Les objets dont on a le moins besoin sont ceux qui charment le plus." Later in his Preface to *Mademoiselle de Maupin* (1835) Gautier extended his theories, maintaining that "les choses sont belles en proportion inverse de leur utilité. Il n'y a de vraiment beau que ce qui ne peut servir à rien. Tout ce qui est utile est laid."

It was Gautier's intention to present an alternative program to that of Victor Hugo and the French Romantics, in whom he found false sentimentality, excessive subjectivity and an irrational enthusiasm for the Middle Ages, all of which he found utterly distasteful. Unlike Hugo who believed that art had "une mission nationale, une mission sociale, une mission humaine," Gautier maintained that literature ought to be completely independent of political and social considerations, and he emphasized his point of view by writing on subjects which had little relation with either. Thus *Mademoiselle de Maupin* is a bizarre novel about a woman who, dressed as a man, inspires the love of D'Albert who believes he must be turning homosexual, succumbing to the charms of a person he takes to be male. This situation is further complicated by D'Albert's mistress Rosette, who also falls in love with Mademoiselle de Maupin, believing her to be a man, and the transvestite herself returns the affection of both her lovers. At the end of the novel the heroine spends part of the night with D'Albert and the rest of it with Rosette, revealing her true sex to both of them and suggesting that they try to love each other because they have both been in love with her. As a narrative Gautier's novel is not very effective. The basic situation is hardly credible, and none of the characters bear the slightest resemblance to real people. Yet this was precisely Gautier's intention, for his main concern was to use this far-fetched plot simply as a vehicle for displaying his talent as a descriptive artist and promulgating his aesthetic credo.

Accustomed to the quasi-realism and vapid platitudes of French Romanticism, Gautier's public found his novel distasteful, and Eugene Mason, one of the more minor English poets of the *fin-de-siècle*, voiced the commonly held opinion of his contemporaries when in a poem entitled "After Reading 'Mlle. de Maupin'," included in his first volume of verse *Flamma Vestalis* (1895), he described Gautier's work with these words:

> Yea, though the carven work be fair and good,
> The arches shapely, and the rich shrine dim,
> Though through the silence steals a perfect hymn
> And all be wrought in Art's divinest mood,
> Yet think not that the goddess deigns to brood
> Above the altar reared and decked by him
> To whom the body's beauty, white and slim,
> Is all the fair and true of womanhood.
>
> A woman's love is other than you deem,
> And only those are worthy of the prize
> Who mate high living with a noble creed;
> Who strive by self-control and tender deed

To catch the spirit-love which never dies
When flesh is clean forgotten as a dream.

Considering the response to *Mademoiselle de Maupin,* it is hardly surprising that the art for art's sake movement as a whole came to be looked upon both in France and in England as simply the rallying cry for those who sought to excuse their excessive interest in subjects abnormal and vicious. Yet Pater seems to have had in mind the correct meaning of the term when in the Conclusion to his *Studies in the History of the Renaissance* (1873) he expressed his belief in the supremacy of art over all other forms of human activity. At first, though, he appears to be advocating little more than a rather crude *carpe diem* approach to life. He tells us, for example, that "not the fruit of experience, but experience itself" is the proper end of existence. We are on this earth for so little time, therefore it behoves us to live intensely, "to burn always with [a] hard gemlike flame." Some spend their lives in "listlessness," others in the "high passions," but, says Pater, "the wisest spend it in art and song":

> For our one chance lies in expanding that interval, in getting as many pulsations as possible into the given time. Great passions may give us this quickened sense of life, ecstasy and sorrow of love, the various forms of enthusiastic activity, disinterested or otherwise, which come naturally to many of us. Of such wisdom, the poetic passion, the desire of beauty, the love of art for its own sake, has most. For art comes to you proposing frankly to give nothing but the highest quality to your moments as they pass, and simply for those moments' sake.

Read out of context it appears that Pater is recommending to his readers that they gather their rosebuds while they may. Read in context it is clear that this was not Pater's intention at all. What he really said was that art can, as it were, confirm one's own conception of morality. We have so little time "to make theories about those things we see and touch." Furthermore, "any theory or ideal or system which requires of us the sacrifice of any or part of this experience, in consideration of some abstract theory we have not identified with ourselves, or of what is only conventional, has no real claim on us." A far more reliable guide is art, which evokes a "quickened and multiplied consciousness" and widens man's sensibilities. Philosophy, said Pater, in the essay on Winckelmann, simply serves culture, "not by the fancied gift of absolute or transcendental knowledge, but by suggesting questions which help one to detect the passion, and strangeness, and dramatic contrasts of life." Art, however, is superior because it alone can communicate the fullness of the world; hence its supreme importance.

Although this seems to have been Pater's philosophy, many writers of the Nineties either misunderstood or willfully ignored the fact that his theories were based on traditional ethics. Oscar Wilde, for example, who in *De Profundis* (1897) declared that the *Renaissance* had exerted a tremendous influence on his life, interpreted its conclusion quite simply as a plea for liberty in all matters of experience and expression, as evidenced by his glorification of the "new hedonism" in *Dorian Gray* and the details of his personal career.

It is tempting to blame Wilde entirely for his misreading of Pater, but the older critic certainly left himself open to misinterpretation. The voluptuous, slow-moving cadences of his prose, his rich and suggestive imagery, exude a seductive and not altogether wholesome charm which activates the libido rather than stimulates the brain. Neither is Pater's precise meaning always clear. Specifically, in the essay on Winckelmann his comments on the nature of the Hellenic ideal could, and indeed did, suggest that he sanctioned sexual

20

inversion.

In this essay Pater describes the Hellenic ideal, as a state "in which man is at unity with himself, with his physical nature, with the outward world," and demonstrates the eighteenth-century German critic Winckelmann's sympathy with it. He comments upon Wincklemann's close friendships with young men which, says Pater, brought him "into contact with this pride of human form, and stirring the thoughts with its bloom perfected in reconciliation to this spirit of Greek sculpture." The dangers implicit in Pater's remarks about Winckelmann for sensitive and impressionable young men are all too obvious, and they are heightened by Pater's unwillingness to cast upon the German moral blame. On the contrary, he points out that it was precisely because Wincklemann's nature and temperament were as he describes them that he was able to appreciate fully the Hellenic ideal:

> Occupied ever with himself, perfecting himself and developing his genius, he was not content, as so often happens with such natures, that the atmosphere between him and other minds should be thick and clouded; he was ever jealously refining his meaning into a form, express, clear, objective. This temperament he matured and invigorated by friendships which kept him always in direct contact with the spirit of youth.

And so he was able to maintain his instinctual, vital appreciation of the Hellenic ideal.

The organic unity of Hellenic art and literature was attractive to writers of the time, and John Addington Symonds, for one, was irresistibly drawn to it. In his final chapter to *Studies of the Greek Poets* (1873-76), for example, he suggested that the Greeks had something to teach the nineteenth century about morality. Symonds asserts that the Greeks viewed man as an organic part of the universe, which he claimed was an intuitive insight now scientifically established by the theory of evolution. Therefore, says Symonds, as it is now proved that man acts in accordance with certain fixed laws, it is clear that "the very seat of our supposed liberty, our desires and personal peculiarities, distinctive tastes and special predilections, are determined for us in great measure by circumstances beyond our control." Hence,

> Can we not in this way venture to anticipate that the men of the future may obtain demonstrated certainty with regard to man considered as an integral part of the universe, that they may understand the conditions of his conduct as clearly as we now apprehend the behaviour of certain gases, and that their problems will be, not how to check healthy normal appetites, but how to multiply and fortify faculties? Can we not dream that morality will be one branch of the study of the world as a whole, a department of Yὰ φνοzκά, when Φύσις, regarded as a total unity, that suffers no crude distinction of mind and body, has absorbed our scientific attention?

Symonds' homo-erotic tendencies also found expression in verse, as, for example, in the poems included in his collection of essays *In the Key of Blue* (1892). Other poets, too, wrote rapturously of the beauty of young men and the delights of boy-love: Oscar Wilde, Marc André Raffalovich, the Reverend E.E. Bradford, John Gambril Nicholson, Baron Corvo, Edward Cracroft Lefroy and Theodore Wratislaw, for example. Lefroy was perhaps an innocent, and his poems "A Cricket Bowler," "A Football Player," and "Bill: A Portrait," merely the guileless effusions of a pre-Freudian Anglican clergyman. Nicholson's poems, however, are blatantly homosexual. Whatever Wratislaw's sexual proc-

22

livities may have been, it is certain that his poem "To a Sicilian Boy," announced in the table of contents of his volume *Caprices* (1893) but omitted from the text, was an undisguised if artistically indifferent expression of Uranian sentiments:

> Love, I adore the contours of thy shape,
> Thine exquisite breast and arms adorable;
> The wonders of thy heavenly throat compel
> Such fire of love as even my dreams escape:
> I love thee as the sea-foam loves the cape,
> Or as the shore the sea's enchanting spell:
> In sweets the blossoms of thy mouth excel
> The tenderest bloom of peach or purple grape.
>
> I love thee, sweet! Kiss me, again, again!
> Thy kisses soothe me as tired earth the rain;
> Between thine arms I find mine only bliss:
> Ah! let me in thy bosom still enjoy
> Oblivion of the past, divinest boy,
> And the dull ennui of a woman's kiss!

The closing chapter of Symonds' *Studies of the Greek Poets* was little more than an apologia for sexual inversion, as many of his readers were quick to see, and it was hardly surprising that the book was not adopted at Clifton School, as Symonds had hoped. Pater also came under fire, and realising that he had gone too far, or, perhaps, through excessive naiveté had laid himself open to misinterpretation, he endeavored to make amends. Reviewing Oscar Wilde's *The Picture of Dorian Gray* in *The Bookman* of November 1891, he pointed out that the true Epicurean, like his own Marius, aimed at a "complete though harmonious development of man's entire organism," and did not seek to subdue his "moral sense." But it was too late. Wilde's distortion of

Pater's doctrine, no less than Symonds', was accepted as a true reflection of the critic's intentions, and although as early as 1877 Pater had even gone as far as to suppress the Conclusion to the second edition of *Studies in the History of the Renaissance*, he could not call his disciples back to the truth. Believing that it was Pater's intention to advocate the cultivation of all life's joys and sins, his young followers turned to subjects hitherto regarded as unmentionable, and loosed a torrent of literature which exalted the perverse and glorified the exotic.

Besides poetry of a *musa puerilis* cast, the Decadents were also pre-occupied with fatal women, seductive vampires who brought disaster to those who fell under their enchantment. Frequently, these creatures were portrayed as music hall artistes, as in poems such as Symons' "La Mélinite: Moulin Rouge," included in *Silhouettes* (1892). Sometimes, as in Richard Le Gallienne's "Beauty Accurst," from *English Poems* (1894) they are represented as supernatural beings with magical powers of ludicrous proportions:

> I AM so fair that wheresoe'er I wend
> Men yearn with strange desire to kiss my face,
> Stretch out their hands to touch me as I pass,
> And women follow me from place to place.
>
> A poet writing honey of his dear
> Leaves the wet page,—ah! leaves it long to dry.
> The bride forgets it is her marriage-morn,
> The bridegroom too forgets as I go by.
>
> Within the street where my strange feet shall stray
> All markets hush and traffickers forget,
> In my gold head forget their meaner gold,
> The poor man grows unmindful of his debt.
>
> Two lovers kissing in a secret place,

Should I draw nigh,—will never kiss again;
I come between the king and his desire,
  And where I am all loving else is vain.

Lo! when I walk along the woodland way
  Strange creatures leer at me with uncouth love
And from the grass reach upward to my breast,
  And to my mouth lean from the boughs above.

The sleepy kine move round me in desire
  And press their oozy lips upon my hair,
Toads kiss my feet and creatures of the mire,
  The snails will leave their shells to watch me there.

But all this worship, what is it to me?
  I smite the ox and crush the toad in death:
I only know I am so very fair,
  And that the world was made to give me breath.

I only wait the hour when God shall rise
  Up from the star where he so long hath sat,
And bow before the wonder of my eyes
  And set me there—I am so fair as that.

Though Arnold, Symonds, and to a greater extent Pater, provided the Decadents with theoretical justification for their modes of writing, other English writers in some measure anticipated their keen interest in the exotic and the bizarre. As Mario Praz has shown in *The Romantic Agony*, such subjects as algolagnia, perverse and destructive love, and the desire for death and oblivion, had all been essential ingredients of the Romantic Movement, most notably in the poetry of Keats and Coleridge, whose "La Belle Dame Sans Merci" and "Christabel" respectively, portrayed the type of fatal woman who was to achieve eminence in the Decadent poetry of the Nineties. Such aspects of the Romantic Movement had been perpetuated in the writings of Swinburne, Dante Gabriel Rossetti and the Pre-Raphaelites, and as early as 1871 critics were complaining of the lubricious character of contemporary society and literature.

Thus, in his rabid essay entitled "The Fleshly School of Poetry," published in the *Contemporary Review* in 1871, Robert Buchanan described the age as a cesspool of carnality and degradation. Everywhere, he wrote, "sensualism was shooting its ulcerous roots deeper and deeper, blotching more and more the fair surface of things." As for contemporary poets: Swinburne left Buchanan's "mind jaded, [his] whole body sick and distressed, a dull pain lurking in the region of the medulla oblongata," while in Rossetti he heard "only the heated ravings of an affected lover, indecent for the most part, and often blasphemous."

Buchanan, of course, exaggerates the degradation of his age and its most notable poets, yet there is some truth in his remarks. Before Swinburne's *Poems and Ballads* (1866), England had not witnessed such a display of outspoken enthusiasm for the darker sins since the Restoration, and clearly both Swinburne and Rossetti helped to prepare the ground for the English Decadence, although it may be argued whether or not they planted the seeds. One of the reasons for the difficulty in assessing the debt the Decadents owed to such poets as Swinburne and Rossetti is the fact that Swinburne, especially, shared the Decadents' enthusiasm for the writings of Gautier and Baudelaire, and it is not always clear whether the Decadents came to these writers directly, or after they had been filtered through Swinburne. There is little doubt, however, that the English poet stimulated the Decadents' interest in the more lurid aspects of nineteenth-century French literature, and certainly much of Swinburne's work afforded precedent for the later poets' treatment of the exotic and the perverse.

Swinburne's admiration for both Gautier and Baudelaire is obvious. He was author of some "Memorial Verses on the Death of Théophile Gautier;" he composed a sonnet praising *Mademoiselle de Maupin* as the "golden book of spirit and sense/The holy writ of beauty;" and it is clear that both his *Chronicle of Tebaldo Tebaldei*, an unfinished prose work written in 1861, and the later *Lesbia Brandon*, written around 1866 but not published until 1957, were strongly influenced by the novel itself. In 1862 Swinburne had published a laudatory article on Baudelaire in *The Spectator*, while in *Poems and Ballads* (1866) such pieces as "Laus Veneris," "Dolores," "Anactoria" and "The Leper" reflect some of the perverse subjects and themes characteristic of *Les Fleurs du Mal*. Finally, in "Ave Atque Vale," included in the series of *Poems and Ballads* (1878), Swinburne recorded his admiration for Baudelaire in a particularly fulsome elegy occasioned by the premature announcement of the poet's death. "The lord of light," the poet writes,

> Makes manifest his music and his might
> In hearts that open and in lips that soften
> With the soft flame and heat of songs that shine.
> Thy lips indeed he touched with bitter wine,
> And nourished them indeed with bitter bread;
> Yet surely from his hand thy soul's food came,
> The fire that scarred thy spirit at his flame
> Was lighted, and thine hungering heart he fed
> Who feeds our hearts with fame.

However, in spite of Swinburne's awareness of the mystical side of the French poet's genius, whether he fully understood Baudelaire is open to question.

Like Gautier, Baudelaire was concerned with shocking a complacent public out of its mindless composure, and also like Gautier he intended to make clear that art had no obligation to society but was instead superior to it. However, where Gautier had been content merely to assert the autonomy of art, Baudelaire justified its superiority by pointing out that man and nature, sin and virtue, were only understandable in relation to the antithesis of the natural and the artificial. As he wrote in "Eloge du Maquillage" (1860), a woman uses cosmetics to transcend her natural ugliness, and in a similar way the poet attempts to create beauty from the sordid materials of the world about him.

Following Swedenborg, Baudelaire subscribed to the Platonic idea of the universal analogy between the natural and the spiritual worlds, believing that a beautiful poem not only affirms the existence of an ideal state, but that the physical manifestations of the natural world have their counterparts in a transcendental state as well, a theory he expressed in his poem "Correspondances."

> La nature est un temple où les vivants piliers
> Laissent parfois sortir de confuses paroles;
> L'homme y passe à travers des forêts de symboles
> Qui l'observent avec des regards familiers.
>
> Comme de longs échos qui de loin se confondent
> Dans une ténébreuse et profonde unité,
> Vaste comme la nuit et comme la clarté,
> Les parfums, les couleurs et les sons se répondent.

Man himself was a weak debased creature, obsessed with the inevitability of his damnation, yet stirred by aspirations towards goodness; and it was this contradiction of forces which accounted for his torment and despair. As Baudelaire wrote in "Le Voyage":

> O Mort, vieux capitaine, il est temps! levons l'ancre!
> Ce pays nous enuie, O Mort! Appareillons!

Si le ciel et la mer sont noirs comme de l'encre
Nos cœurs que tu connais sont remplis de rayons!

Consequently, the only possible relief is death:

Verse-nous ton poison pour qu'il nous réconforte!
Nous voulons, tant ce feu nous brûle le cerveau,
Plonger au fond du gouffre, Enfer ou Ciel, qu'importe?
Au fond de l'Inconnu pour trouver du *nouveau*.

If this is the "real" Baudelaire, Swinburne seemed only minimally interested. It is true that in his *Spectator* article of 1862 he drew attention to Baudelaire's "morality" and his ability to find "beauty in loathsome bodily putrescence and decay," but in the verses of *Poems and Ballads* (1866) it is clear that, for Swinburne, Baudelaire's main attraction was his ability to portrary vice and depravity with a seductive charm.

Though one may understand Buchanan's reaction to *Poems and Ballads*, it is less easy to see why he should have been so incensed by the work of Dante Gabriel Rossetti. It is true that in his poem "Jenny" Rossetti addresses a prostitute, and much of the poem's descriptive detail is undeniably sensuous; but here the poet seems equally concerned with moralising that man's lust is responsible for the woman's downfall, as he is in providing erotic titillation. It is also true that Rossetti's portraits of tubercular, swan-necked women have a rather ambiguous and none too healthy charm, but in his most famous poem, "The Blessed Damosel," and in the equally well known sonnet sequence, "The House of Life," the kind of love the poet celebrates is the harmonious and blessed union between souls and bodies. Yet it was this last work which was responsible for Buchanan's attack.

Unlike Swinburne's, however, Rossetti's debt to Gautier and Baudelaire seems to be slight. That Rossetti knew of

29

Gautier is certain. In 1867 Adah Isaacs Menken, the beautiful American actress and equestrienne, who achieved fame in London by galloping around Astley's Apmhitheatre clad in tights and a leopard skin in an attempted recreation of Mazeppa's ride, deliberately sought out the English poet, having been advised by Gautier that Rossetti was worth cultivating. Later, in 1868, Swinburne in his *Notes on Some Pictures of 1868*, compared Rossetti's *Lilith* to the heroine of Gautier's novel *Mademoiselle de Maupin*, but whether Rossetti was especially influenced by the French writer's work is not clear. Rossetti certainly knew of Baudelaire, for he made a gift of *Fleurs du Mal* to Swinburne in 1864, but again it is doubtful whether Rossetti was much influenced by his writings. Indeed, Rossetti's interest in French poetry seems to have been slight, so much so that when William Rossetti introduced his brother's *Collected Poems* in 1870 he declared that the only French poets whom Dante Gabriel knew were Victor Hugo and Alfred de Musset.

Clearly, Swinburne and Rossetti helped to prepare the way for the Decadents, and as one might expect, there are echoes of the older poets in *fin-de-siècle* verse. Lord Alfred Douglas's "Garden of Death" owes something to Swinburne's "Garden of Proserpine," and in Wilde's "The Sphinx," the loose, richly loaded lines recall Swinburne's most characteristic verse. Symons' early poetry certainly owes much to Rossetti, and, more generally, Yeats noted in his *Autobiography* that Rossetti, together with Pater, was one of the main sources of inspiration for the Rhymers, the former's portrait of Lilith representing for them the idealization of womanhood. On the whole though, indebtedness to Swinburne and Rossetti is less marked than one would perhaps expect: the most clearly demonstrable influence seems to have come directly from France.

As we have seen, Swinburne was the first English poet

of the nineteenth century to draw heavily for inspiration on the literature of France, but his example was quickly followed by two poets in particular, John Payne and Arthur O'Shaughnessy. Payne was an ardent disciple of French literature, and in 1878 translated *The Poems of Master François Villon*, another poet fashionable in the Nineties. Later he produced the more ambitious, five-volume *Flowers from France* (1906-1914) in which he gave English readers a sampling of the more famous French poets in translation; his literary preferences are clearly indicated by his allotting two volumes to the poetry of the nineteenth century, but only one each to the thirteenth and fourteenth centuries, the fifteenth and sixteenth, and the seventeenth and eighteenth centuries. He also became first an admirer and later a friend of Mallarmé, being one of the earliest people in England to appreciate this difficult and at that time widely misunderstood poet. Payne's own poetry reveals his enthusiasm for nineteenth-century French literature too, and in his most accomplished volume, *Songs of Life and Death* (1877), dedicated to the darling of the French Symbolists, the musician and composer Richard Wagner, one can trace the influence of such writers as Aloysius Bertrand, de Sénancourt, Lamennais, Gautier, Baudelaire and Théodore de Banville, whose preoccupation with the *ballade* he faithfully reflects. The predominant tone of the volume is a mournful lyricism.

The same note and a similar enthusiasm for the contemporary literature of France are apparent also in the verses of Payne's friend, Arthur O'Shaughnessy, a poet who suffered the death of his wife and two daughters, and during his own short life hovered on the periphery of the Rossetti circle. Like Payne, O'Shaughnessy's most distinctive note is tuneful melancholy, and he also shares an interest in the doctrine of art for art's sake, as is apparent from the poem entitled simply "Ode" from *Music and Moonlight* (1874), his most

31

distinguished volume:

> We are the music makers,
> And we are the dreamers of dreams,
> Wandering by the lone sea-breakers,
> And sitting by desolate streams;—
> World-losers and world-forsakers,
> On whom the pale moon gleams;
> Yet we are the movers and shakers
> Of the world for ever, it seems.
>
> With wonderful deathless ditties
> We build up the world's great cities,
> And out of a fabulous story
> We fashion an empire's glory;
> One man with a dream, at pleasure,
> Shall go forth and conquer a crown;
> And three with a new song's measure
> Can trample a kingdom down.
>
> We, in the ages lying
> In the buried past of the earth,
> Built Nineveh with our singing,
> And Babel itself in our mirth;
> And o'erthrew them with prophesying
> To the old of the new world's worth;
> For each age is a dream that is dying,
> Or one that is coming to birth.

IV

THERE IS THUS ample evidence for regarding the Decadent poets of the Nineties as heirs to an English Romantic tradition, fortified with borrowings from Gautier, and Baudelaire, and sanctified by the aesthetic theorizing of Walter Pater. In the 'eighties and 'nineties, however, the influence from France became even more marked, giving the Decadent poetry at the end of the century a distinct exoticism. Thus it may be argued that the English Decadence was not so much a new departure as an intensification of existing practices. Later poets still paid lip service to the cult of art for art's sake, they still took inspiration from Baudelaire, but to these were added imitation of prevailing French techniques.

It is obvious, for example, that towards the end of the century a number of English poets followed the technical precepts associated with that group of French writers known as the Parnassians. As we have seen, Gautier had insisted that art had little or nothing to do with the transitory, mundane matters associated with man's social and political institutions, that the only permanency in an impermanent world is art. It followed, therefore, that the artist should strive to make his creations as perfect as possible, for only by so doing could he hope to achieve a measure of eternity. For the writer, Gautier stressed the relationship he felt should exist between literature and the plastic arts, and demanded that the poet lavish his craftsman's skill on the achievement of perfect form and clarity of outline, as a sculptor would hew a shape from a block of marble. This theory he embodied in a collection of poems called *Emaux et Camées* (1853), the very title of which indicates the poet's intentions, and in the last poem of the 1857 edition of that volume set forth his credo under the title "L'Art," which Austin Dobson freely translated in 1876 under the title "Ars Victrix":

> Yes: when the ways oppose—
> When the hard means rebel,
> Fairer the work out-grows,—
> More potent far the spell.

O Poet, then, forbear
The loosely-sandalled verse,
Choose rather thou to wear
The buskin—strait and terse;

Leave to the tiro's hand
The limp and shapeless style,
See that thy form demand
The labour of the file.

Sculptor, do thou discard
The yielding clay,—consign
To Paros marble hard
The beauty of thy line;—

Model thy Satyr's face
For bronze of Syracuse;
In the veined agate trace
The profile of thy muse.

Painter, that still must mix
But transient tints anew,
Thou in the furnace fix
The firm enamel's hue;

Let the smooth tile receive
Thy dove-drawn Erycine;
Thy sirens blue at eve
Coiled in a wash of wine.

All passes. ART alone
Enduring stays to us;
The bust outlasts the throne,—
The Coin, Tiberius;

Even the gods must go;
Only the lofty Rhyme

ILLUSTRATIONS

Joe Haynes and Little Dot Hetherington at the Old Bedford Music Hall by Walter
Sickert.

Derby Day by William Powell Frith.

Bubbles by John Everett Millais.

Nocturne in Black and Gold by James Abbott McNeill Whistler.

Lady Lilith by Dante Gabriel Rossetti.

John Lane (1854-1925)

Aubrey Beardsley's cover design for the first issue of *The Yellow Book*, a journal which acquired a reputation for being one of the most characteristic products of the Decadent Nineties, largely as a result of Beardsley's art work.

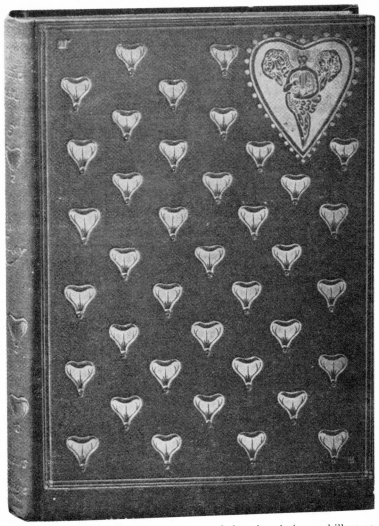

Among the artists whom John Lane commissioned to design and illustrate
his books was Charles Ricketts (1866-1931), who was later elected R.A.
in 1938. His cover design for Lord de Tabley's *Poems: Dramatic and Lyrical*
(1893) is typical of his work for the Bodley Head.

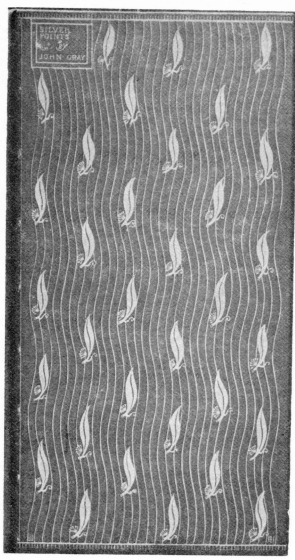

Charles Ricketts was also responsible for the cover design and initial lettering (above and opposite) of John Gray's *Silverpoints* (1893), one of the most characteristic of the Bodley Head's productions.

FLEURS. IMITATED FROM THE
FRENCH
OF
STEPHANE MALLARMÉ

HE *tawny iris—oh! the slim-necked*
swan;
And, sign of exiled souls, the bay
divine;
Ruddy as seraph's heel its fleckless
sheen,
Blushing the brightness of a trampled dawn.

The hyacinth; the myrtle's sweet alarm;
Like to a woman's flesh, the cruel rose,
Blossom'd Herodiade of the garden close,
Fed with ferocious dew of blooddrops warm.

Thou mad'st the lilies' pallor, nigh to swoon,
Which, rolling billows of deep sighs upon,
Through the blue incense of horizons wan,
Creeps dreamily towards the weeping moon.

Praise in the censers, praise upon the gong,
Madone! from the garden of our woes:
On eves celestial throb the echo long!
Ecstatic visions! radiance of haloes!

Mother creatrice! in thy strong, just womb,
Challices nodding the not distant strife;
Great honey'd blossoms, a balsamic tomb
For weary poets blanched with starless life.

XXIX

47

Charles Ricketts' cover design for John Addington Symonds' collection of essays and poems *In the Key of Blue* (1892), published by the Bodley Head.

Leonard Smithers (1861-1907).

ORCHIDS

POEMS

BY

THEODORE WRATISLAW

LEONARD SMITHERS
ARUNDEL STREET: STRAND
LONDON W.C.
1896

Theodore Wratislaw's *Orchids* (1896), printed at the Chiswick Press,
a typical product of Smithers' publishing house.

Not countless years o'erthrow,—
Not long array of time.

Paint, chisel, then, or write;
But, that the word surpass,
With the hard fashion fight,—
With the resisting mass.

Gautier's artfully chiseled lyrics and sharply defined images inspired, first, several poets in France who, calling themselves Parnassians, attempted to follow Gautier's precepts in verses of their own. Later, a number of poets in England— notably Andrew Lang, Austin Dobson and Edmund Gosse—followed suit. None of these poets could properly be called Decadents, but other poets of the time who have greater claim to the title, were also influenced by the Parnassian example, most notably Lionel Johnson. Johnson published in *The Hobby Horse* of 1891 an essay entitled "A Note Upon the Practice and Theory of Verse at the Present Time Obtaining in France," in which he contrasted the grand but technically sloppy effects of such great English poets as Shakespeare and Robert Browning with the more precise artistry of the Parnassians. In his poetry, also, he strove to emulate the Parnassians, writing verse which Ezra Pound in his introduction to *The Poetical Works of Lionel Johnson* (1915) compared to "small slabs of ivory, firmly combined and contrived," as for example in "Dead," singled out by Pound for special praise:

In Merioneth, over the sad moor
  Drives the rain, the cold wind blows:
  Past the ruinous church door,
The poor procession without music goes.

Lonely she wandered out her hour, and died.
  Now the mournful curlew cries

Over her, laid down beside
Death's lonely people: lightly down she lies.

In Merioneth, the wind lives and wails,
  On from hill to lonely hill:
  Down the loud, triumphant gales,
A spirit cries *Be strong!* and cries *Be still!*

Though Parnassianism exerted a powerful influence on the poetry of the English Decadence, a number of poets of the time were equally intoxicated by the more nebulous effects and delicate half-tones of Paul Verlaine, Baudelaire's spiritual successor. Like Baudelaire, Verlaine found the world a depressing place, and though he did not rail as loudly, he too looked upon life as a melancholy *danse macabre*. Unlike Baudelaire , however, whose preoccupation with the artificial was justified in terms of his aesthetic doctrine, Verlaine seems to have been drawn to it by a pathological fascination. His poetic sensibility responded to the melancholy half-tones of the twilit city and encouraged him to seek always for *la nuance* rather than for the color itself. For Verlaine, in so far as he was interested in the spirit world, a transcendental state was not so much to be perceived through the objects of physical reality as evoked by the music of poetry. As he wrote in "Art Poétique," as translated by Symons:

Music first and foremost of all!
Choose your measure of odd not even,
Let it melt in the air of heaven,
Pose not, poise not, but rise and fall.

Choose your words, but think not whether
Each to other of old belong:
What so dear as the dim grey song
Where clear and vague are joined together?

'Tis veils of beauty for beautiful eyes,
'Tis the trembling light of the naked noon
'Tis the medley of blue and gold, the moon
And stars in the cool of autumn skies.

Let every shape of its shade be born;
Colour, away! come to me, shade!
Only of shade can the marriage be made
Of dream with dream and of flute with horn.

Shun the Point, lest death with it come,
Unholy laughter and cruel wit
(For the eyes of the angels weep at it)
And all the garbage of the scullery-scum.

Take Eloquence, and wring the neck of him!
You had better, by force, from time to time,
Put a little sense in the head of Rhyme:
If you watch him not, you will be at the beck of him.

O, who shall tell us the wrongs of Rhyme?
What witless savage or what deaf boy
Has made for us this twopenny toy
Whose bells ring hollow and out of time?

Music always and music still!
Let your verse be a wandering thing
That flutters in flight from a soul on the wing
Towards other skies at a new whim's will.

Let your verse be the luck of the lure
Afloat on the winds that at morning hint
Of the odours of thyme and the savour of mint—
And all the rest is literature.

Verlaine, then, cultivated the vague and avoided direct
statement in favor of indirect moods and sensations. For

him the "impression" mattered: only through the impression
could the spirit of beauty be experienced. His views were
followed by a number of the Decadent poets of the Nineties,
by Ernest Dowson, John Gray and in particular by Arthur
Symons, whose "Music and Memory," from *Silhouettes*
(1892), is one of the most typical "impressionist" poems of
the period:

> Across the tides of music, in the night,
> Her magical face,
> A light upon it as the happy light
> Of dreams in some delicious place
> Under the moonlight in the night.
>
> Music, soft throbbing music in the night,
> Her memory swims
> Into the brain, a carol of delight;
> The cup of music overbrims
> With wine of memory, in the night.
>
> Her face across the music, in the night,
> Her face a refrain,
> A light that sings along the waves of light,
> A memory that returns again,
> Music in Music, in the night.

Unlike Parnassianism, however, which was well entren-
ched before the end of the century, and endured through the
early years of the twentieth to become an essential part of
the Imagists' creed, Impressionism was something of a fad
which all but expired with the Decadence. During the
Nineties, however, it was very much in vogue, and Verlaine
himself came to be regarded as a martyred saint who died
in the cause of beauty, the victim of a crass and unfeeling
bourgeoisie who were deaf to his music and saw only the
sordidness of his life.

Decadent Poetry

Gautier and the Parnassians, Baudelaire and Verlaine all left their mark on the English Decadence, but the most important foreign influence of all was not a poet but the novelist Joris-Karl Huysmans, whose *A Rebours* (1884), described by Symons as the "breviary" of the Decadent Movement, gave many of the Decadents their *raison d'être*. It was one thing to subscribe to the theory of art for art's sake or to copy the technical idiosyncrasies of certain French writers; but to model oneself on the spectacular career of des Esseintes, the hero of Huysmans' notorious novel, became almost obligatory for those who sought membership among the Decadent élite. In *A Rebours*, des Esseintes, wearied and disgusted by life, withdraws from society, preferring the seclusion of his sumptuously furnished apartment on the outskirts of Paris to the hubbub of the city. There, in this solitary retreat, he systematically cultivates his passion for the bizarre and the exotic, reading the works of the Greek and Latin Decadence, fondling jewels, composing "symphonies of perfumes," and tending rare and exotic plants, hoping to find in these pursuits some justification for existence. At last, his nervous system on the point of collapse, he is forced to recognize that he has reached a crisis, where only two alternatives remain open to him: a choice in Barbey d'Aurevilly's words, between the muzzle of a pistol or the foot of the Cross.

Comma

Although Huysmans' novel achieved a certain *succès de scandale*, it was not intended simply as a celebration of the perverse and the unnatural. It was, on the contrary, a serious, if ironic, exploration of all the sensuous pleasures life has to offer in the hope of finding in them some justification for existence. Yet, to many, the novel's main attraction was its exhaustive inventory of abnormal pleasures (a catalogue made doubly attractive by the artificial prose style in which it was written), which served as a stimulus to those

55

who aspired to the Decadent ideal. Certainly these were the qualities which appealed most readily to Dorian Gray, and, we may infer, to Wilde himself. In Dorian Gray Wilde alludes to Husymans' *A Rebours*, and describes it in some detail:

> It was the strangest book Dorian had ever read. It seemed to him that in exquisite movement, and to the delicate sound of flutes, the sins of the world were passing in dumb show before him. Things of which he had never dreamed were gradually revealed.
>
> It was a novel without a plot, and with only one character, being indeed, simply a psychological study of a young Parisian who spent his life trying to realise in the nineteenth century all the passions and modes of thought that belonged to every century except his own, and to sum up, as it were, in himself the various moods through which the world spirit had ever passed, loving for their mere artificiality those renunciations that men have unwisely called virtue as those natural rebellions that wise men call sin. The style in which it was written was that curious jewelled style, vivid and obscure at once, full of argot and archaisms, of technical expressions and of elaborate paraphrases, that characterises the work of some of the finest artists of the French School of symbolists. There were in it metaphors as monstrous as orchids and as evil in colour. The life of the sense was described in the terms of the mystical philosophy. One hardly knew at times whether one was reading the spiritual ecstasies of some medieval saint or the morbid confessions of a modern sinner. It was a poisonous book. The heavy odour of incense seemed to hang about its pages and trouble the brain. The mere cadence of the sentences, the subtle monotony of the music, so full it was of complex refrains and movements

elaborately repeated, produced in the mind of the lad, a form of reveries, a malady of dreaming, that made him unconscious of the falling day and the creeping shadows.

In Wilde's description of *A Rebours* we have the essential difference between the French and English Decadence. For all their insistence on the separation of art and life and their preoccupation with abnormal subjects, the French were not altogether irresponsible. Their literature was concerned with the possibility of an ideal state which would be of greater value than the bourgeois, materialistic world of conventional behavior and morality. They were, in fact, not so much "Decadents" as "Symbolists," writers who intended to evoke a superior state of being, writers dedicated to "le Beau et l'Idéal." Verlaine himself in an interview with Jules Huret in 1891 dismissed the term "Decadent" as meaningless, complaining that its use gave entirely the wrong idea about his own work and that of his contemporaries.

One cannot say that many of the English Decadents were concerned with ideal values. Certainly a number of them professed to be concerned solely with beauty, and one or two of them seem genuinely to have aspired to a spiritual world which they deemed more satisfying than life here below. W.B. Yeats, for example, in the Nineties at least, though he was to modify his position later, believed that poetry would become a "poetry of essences, separated one from another in little and intense poems," the result of "an ever more arduous search for an almost disembodied ecstasy." He also believed that the poet "should seek out those wavering, meditative, organic rhythms, which are the embodiment of the imagination, that neither desires nor hates, because it has done with time, and only wishes to gaze upon some reality, some beauty." Lionel Johnson, similarly dissatisfied with a purely earthbound existence, looked to the Roman

Catholic Church to provide him with spiritual sustenance. For most of their contemporaries, however, it was not so much transcendence they sought as escape. Thus, when Ernest Dowson at the close of his "Nuns of the Perpetual Adoration" reminded us that "our roses fade, the world is wide; / But there, beside the altar, there is rest," he voiced an imperfectly conceived death-wish rather than a strenuously held belief in the spirit. By contrast, Baudelaire, Huysmans, and perhaps even Verlaine, for all their evident concern with sensuality and eroticism, were nonetheless fundamentally mystical in their approach to life.

V

INDEED, for all their enthusiasm for contemporary French literature, the English Decadents failed almost completely to appreciate its ultimate intentions. They acknowledged the French writers' emphasis on style, and sought to embody the same technical precision in their own work, sometimes attempting to reduplicate the finely wrought, sculptured images of Gautier and the Parnassians, and at other times, fortified by the example of the painter Whistler's hazy "nocturnes," strove for the vague imprecision of Verlaine. They leaned heavily towards Verlaine's idea of the supreme value of music, and sought to imitate his rhythms, often with success. Most obviously, however, they took inspiration from those subjects exploited by Verlaine and Baudelaire: the charm of the artificial; the attraction of the city in all its aspects; the fascination of mysterious and beautiful women. Finally, the melancholy of Verlaine, and the *weltschmerz* of Baudelaire were adopted, but mainly as an artistic pose. While there are plenty of sighs and similar expressions of despair in

English Decadent poetry, the general effect is more of a petulant moan than the cry of deeply experienced disillusionment.

The English Decadence is a very feeble echo of the plaintive cry across the Channel. Unlike the French Decadence, which had matured over a period of seventy years or so and had been dedicated for the most part to definite artistic ideals, the majority of the writers in the English Decadent tradition were prompted mainly by a spirit of revolt, and lacking an aesthetic of their own, simply copied what they regarded as the salient characteristics of a similar movement in France.

Thus, although most of the English Decadents professed to share the Continental writers' belief in the importance of music in relation to poetry, they seem not to have been fully aware of the doctrine's implications. In France, both Verlaine and Mallarmé had stressed the significance of "music" in literature. For Verlaine, as A.G. Lehmann has pointed out in *The Symbolist Aesthetic in France* (1948), music seems to have meant little more than audible harmony, mellifluous cadences which fall pleasingly on the ear, while Mallarmé seems to have understood the word to refer to an inaudible harmony, a sort of music of the spheres, a Platonic ideal to which all poetry aspired. In short, Mallarmé's conception of music seems to have been close to Pater's, as he described it in his essay on "The School of Giorgione" in *Studies in the History of the Renaissance*. There Pater had suggested that "although each art has... its own specific order of impressions and an untranslatable charm... it is noticeable that, in its special mode of handling its given material, each art may be observed to pass into the condition of some other art, by what German critics call *Anders-Streben* —a partial alienation from its own limitations, through which the arts are able, not indeed to supply the place of each other, but reciprocally to lend each other new forces." Thus, "some of the most delightful music seems to be always approaching to figure, to pictorial definition," and "sculpture aspires out of the hard limitation of pure form towards colour, or its equivalent," while "French poetry generally with the art of engraving." But most important:

> *All art constantly aspires to the condition of music.* For while in all other kinds of art it is possible to distinguish the matter from the form, and the understanding can always make this distinction, yet it is the constant effort of art to obliterate it.

To this aesthetic doctrine the majority of the English Decadents paid only partial allegiance. They acknowledged Pater's belief in the ability of the various arts "to lend each other new forces," for Gautier had shown them that poetry could aspire to sculpture; Whistler had demonstrated that painting had affinities with music; and more generally, Baudelaire, in his poem "Correspondances," had asserted the complex interrelation between all things on this earth and those above, a theory which led Swinburne, and after him a few of the Decadents, to explore cautiously the possibilities of synesthesia. Poets such as Wilde and Symons made efforts to capture the pictorial effects of such painters as Whistler, Degas and Watteau in their poetry, and in the following poem called "The Opium Smoker" from *Days and Nights* (1889), Symons handles synesthetic techniques with some assurance:

> I am engulfed and drown deliciously.
> Soft music like a perfume, and sweet light
> Golden with audible odours exquisite,
> Swathe me with the cerements for eternity.
> Time is no more. I pause and yet I flee.

A million ages wrap me round with night.
I drain a million ages of delight.
I hold the future in my memory.

Also I have this garret which I rent,
This bed of straw, and this that was a chair,
This worn-out body like a tattered tent,
This crust, of which the rats have eaten part,
This pipe of opium; rage, remorse, despair;
This soul at pawn and this delirious heart.

Yet the English Decadents seem not to have grasped fully what Mallarmé and Pater had meant by music. Dowson strove to write poems in which the words had been chosen more for their musical qualities than for their sense, and Symons wrote airs for the lute, in which he tried to capture the simplicity of that instrument's tone as well as its melancholy plangency. Perhaps most interesting of all, A.B. Miall prefaced the four sections of his volume *Nocturnes and Pastorals* (1896) with several bars of music from Chopin and Schubert, evidently intending that the music should set the tone for the verse that followed. But almost always the Decadents seem to have had in mind audible music rather than the harmonious interdependence of form and content, which blended together comprise one beautiful, indivisible whole. It was Verlaine rather than Mallarmé they chose as their model, and though both John Gray and Arthur Symons translated the latter with considerable success, and W.B. Yeats was for a time attracted to him too, he was never very popular among the English Decadents, it being left to the generation of T.S. Eliot and Ezra Pound to explore more fully the possibilities of the Mallarméan aesthetic.

VI

A POETRY as heavily derivative as that of the English Decadence revals, not surprisingly, uncertainty of direction; it has, most noticeably, a curiously factititous air. One rarely feels that it has been genuinely inspired, that it is the product of a passionately held conviction or attitude. Indeed, it would be strange if one felt otherwise, for most of the poets associated with the movement seem to have lacked a clearly defined identity of their own. For many, it seems to have been *de rigueur* to ape the attitudes of French literary bohemia. Others aspired to the courtly insouciance of a bygone age, Herbert Horne, for example, looking to the Restoration, and Aubrey Beardsley to the France of Louis XV, for guidance in matters of conduct and also for poetic inspiration. Those who were—or liked to consider themselves—Celts, that is to say W.B. Yeats, Ernest Rhys, Lionel Johnson, Victor Plarr, John Todhunter, regarded Ireland, Wales and even Brittany as their spiritual homes, seeing themselves as nineteenth-century reincarnations of the great mythic bards of the past. But almost without exception the Decadent poets seem to have been intent on establishing suitable identities for themselves rather than developing their own personalities.

Although the Decadents sought everywhere for suitable *personae*, one attitude they all seem to have held in common: they believed that they were the unacknowledged aristocracy of letters. They felt they were above the crowd, aesthetically more refined than their fellows, to whom they refused to pander or conform. Most of them had little contact with the masses, and were antagonistic to the popular movements of the time, desiring to keep the unpleasant realities of everyday life at a distance. The few who did concern themselves with contemporary social problems tended to be social outcasts themselves, impractical idealists with Utopian visions whose reformatory schemes met with little success. Prone to manic depression, their lives were invariably unhappy, when they were made to realise the discrepancy between their dreams for a better world and social reality.

There was the feminist Amy Levy, for example, who contributed a number of poems and some prose to the *Pelican*, a magazine devoted to the cause of Women's Suffrage, and whose volume of verses, *Xantippe and Other Poems* (1881) included a spirited defense by Xantippe of her domestic conduct. She also wrote a number of sad, typically *fin-de-siècle* poems such as "Last Words" in which she insisted that "All's done with utterly, /*All's done with*. Death to me/ Was ever Death indeed;/to me no kindly creed/Consolatory was given." Unlike most of the verses of the Decadents, however, Amy Levy's lyrical apostrophe to death was no empty gesture. She believed in the right of the individual to end his own life, as she made clear in an article she contributed to *The Cambridge Review* in 1884 on the ethics of suicide, and in September 1889, true to her principles, she died by her own hand.

Similar to Amy Levy was the dreamy anarchist John Barlas, an ardent socialist who in between composing melancholy, escapist verses and strident poems on human injustice, demonstrated in Trafalgar Square, incited mill workers at Dundee to revolution, and fired a pistol at the House of Commons to express his contempt for parliamentary procedure. He too came to an unhappy end, dying in Gartnavel Asylum, Glasgow, in 1914.

Thus, for all their apparent involvement with humanity and social injustice, Levy and Barlas were typically Decadent in so far as they seem to have been more inclined to withdraw from life than to take part in it. For the Decadents, withdrawal was almost axiomatic. Their enthusiasm for the elaborate ritual of the Roman Catholic Church, lovingly portrayed in a number of poems by Lionel Johnson, is of course symptomatic of this attitude, and so is the fact that many of the Decadents were confirmed drug-takers, alcoholics or homosexuals. Indeed, the kind of sex that is most frequently celebrated by the Decadents is of a peculiarly negative kind. The object of affection is either a member of the poet's own sex, a sterile androgyna, a child of infinite purity, or a prostitute whose depravity precludes the likelihood of natural human love, and whenever a normal relationship is described, it is usually to record its passing. It is in this psychological context that we should consider the Decadents' love of artifice, whether it takes the form of a painted chorus-girl, the city, or the elaborate and sometimes recondite imagery which some of them affected. Even their poems of seeming artlessness are so self-consciously simple that they frequently appear more artificial and contrived than some of their more elaborate verses.

The Decadents were unable to approach life unless they could cloak it with mystery, or veil it with garments woven from their fanciful dreams. Almost always we sense that their interest in writing poetry is to create dream worlds wherein they can lose themselves and so avoid facing reality. It is hardly surprising, therefore, that the setting of many of the Decadents' poems is the East, the orient of romantic legend, Burton's *Arabian Nights* suffused with exotic perfumes, brilliant with opulent decoration, and peopled by beautiful and delicate young men and maids, who stroll langorously through a melancholy, scented twilight. Even in the writings of the Indian poetess Sarojini Naidu the authentic note is lacking, her poetry reflecting more the Decadents' love of the bizarre and the artificial than actuality, as her "Nightfall in the City of Hyderabad" demonstrates:

See how the speckled sky burns like a pigeon's throat,
Jewelled with embers of opal and peridote.

See the white river that flashes and scintillates,
Curved like a tusk from the mouth of the city-gates.

Hark, from the minaret, how the muezzin's call
Floats like a battle-flag over the city wall

From trellised balconies, languid and luminous
Faces gleam, veiled in a splendour voluminous.

Leisurely elephants wind through the winding lanes,
Swinging their silver bells flung from their silver chains.

Round the high Char Minar sounds of gay cavalcades
Blend with the music of cymbals and serenades.

Over the city bridge Night comes majestical,
Borne like a queen to a sumptuous festival.

The Decadents' inability to face reality is well portrayed
in G.S. Street's *Autobiography of a Boy* (1894), in which Tubby,
the ineffectual hero, after failing to sin extravangantly in
England, is at last exiled to Canada where he imagines he
will make a red sash the keynote to his sartorial scheme,
and strike out for "the forests, or the mountains, or whatever
they are, and try to forget." Street's satiric novel is both an
amusing and effective attack on the Decadents, but perhaps
its most interesting feature lies not in the text itself but in
the imprint, for the novel was published by the Bodley Head,
which had established a reputation by printing the work of
the Decadents. John Lane and Elkin Mathews, partners
of the press, had made it their policy to seek out relatively
unknown writers of distinctly Decadent stamp, with a view
to publishing their work, one of the conditions being that the
authors would forego the privilege of royalties. Furthermore,

Lane and Mathews were also able to economize in matters of printing and binding without impairing the general attractiveness of their volumes, turning out limited editions of handsome little books at very little cost. Typical of their work is John Gray's *Silverpoints* (1893), a book whose general appearance lays greater claim to attention, perhaps, than its contents. It is a tall, slim, handsome volume of thirty-five pages, bound in green cloth, on which a flame design is stamped in gold. The paper is expensive (hand-made Von Gelder), and the issue was limited to 250 copies.

As a safeguard Lane and Mathews continued to publish the work of safer, more established writers—the poetry of William Watson for example—but they soon acquired a reputation for being the leading purveyors of literary Decadence, publishing the verses of Wilde, John Davidson, Lord de Tabley, Laurence Housman, Theo Marzials, John Gray, William Theodore Peters, and most notably, Richard Le Gallienne, whose slender talent found expression in a steady flow of tastefully designed volumes bound in blue buckram. In April, 1894 they began publishing *The Yellow Book*, which was regarded at the time as a distinctly daring magazine, mainly on account of the illustrations by its art-editor, Aubrey Beardsley. Yet as is clear from their willingness to publish G.S. Street's *Autobiography of a Boy*, and their publication of Jocelyn Quilp's *Baron Verdigris: A Romance of the Reversed Direction* (1894), a book dedicated "equally to Fin-de-Sièclism, the sensational novel, and the Drawing-Room Ballad," and Owen Seaman's *Battle of the Bays* (1896), a volume of parodies for the most part directed against the leading Decadent poets, Lane and Mathews seem to have favored the Decadents simply as a commercial proposition. They felt no scruples about publishing simultaneously works belonging to the movement and others attacking it, even going so far as to publish a book-length parody of their favorite author,

Le Gallienne, entitled *The Quest of the Gilt-Edged Girl* (1897) by Richard Le Lyrienne, generally believed to be a pseudonym for David Hodge. Satire on the Decadents was, in short, good advertisement. In 1895, however, after Oscar Wilde had been sentenced to imprisonment for homosexuality, and the public's fairly tolerant attitude towards the Decadents turned to violent opposition, the Bodley Head modified its policy, favoring thereafter less controversial writers.

Another publisher who gave impetus to the English Decadence by making it his policy to publish the work of the Decadents was Leonard Smithers, a barrister who forsook the bar for the book-trade and made a living by the surreptitious printing and sale of erotica. Like the Bodley Head, Smithers too was drawn to the Decadents for reasons other than literary. Perhaps his interest in such writers was less commercial than the Bodley Head's, for though personally and professionally a disciple of Eros, he had a place in his heart for Apollo as well, and occasionally seems to have striven to combine his enthusiasm for the two. It was Smithers who published *The Savoy*, perhaps the best of the many late nineteenth-century aesthetic magazines, and it was he who commissioned most of Beardsley's later work at a time when more cautious publishers would have nothing to do with it. He also published the work of Arthur Symons, Ernest Dowson, Theodore Wratislaw, A. B. Miall and Vincent O'Sullivan, and it was he who had the courage to publish Wilde's *Ballad of Reading Gaol* in 1898, at a time when most people were striving to forget that this writer had ever existed. Nevertheless, even if we grant Smithers some measure of devotion to literary ideals, there is little doubt that like Lane and Mathews his interest in the Decadent Movement was not above all literary.

It was largely due to the efforts of the Bodley Head and

Leonard Smithers that the Decadents were able to reach their public, and though it would be unfair to say that without them the Decadent Movement would never have come into being, it is likely that they contributed in no small measure to its success. The Decadent Movement was, in other words, an artificially cultivated phenomenon, and it is not surprising that it lasted for only a few years, growing feebler as the new century progressed and expiring simultaneously with the first casualties of the 1914-18 war.

Of course those poets who during the 1890's had established themselves as belonging to the Decadent tradition, continued to write in the same vein, but after 1900 only a very few writers began their literary careers by writing in the *fin-de-siècle* mode. Those who did are hardly significant. Among them was Montague Summers, whose *Antinous and Other Poems* (1907) celebrated boy love, and perhaps more interesting there was Edmund John, whose "Salome," included in his first volume of poems, entitled *A Flute of Sardonyx* (1913), is more outrageously perverse than any Salome poem of the Decadent period. Neither of these poets is worth serious critical attention, but they do have some slight documentary significance as late Decadents, poets whose work provides a tenuous link between the 1890's and the Firbankian-Sitwellian 'twenties, when the Decadent mode was self-consciously cultivated for satiric or surrealistic ends.

VII

IT HAS BEEN ARGUED by E.D.H. Johnson in his *Alien Vision of Victorian Poetry* that the three main poets of the Victorian era—Tennyson, Browning and Matthew Arnold—all desired to write poems about their personal experience, yet felt guilty about doing so in the belief that it was the poet's duty to express general truths which would educate and inspirit mankind. For the Victorians this was a conflict comparatively easy to resolve. The poet had a duty which it would be wrong to ignore; he had been granted insight and the power to express his vision, and if he were to fulfill his role as a useful member of society he had no choice other than to communicate those experiences which would be understood and appreciated by all. The Decadents, on the other hand, were not at all sure that society deserved, or indeed was capable of understanding, what the poet had to say, and preferred simply to give expression to whatever passing fancy they pleased. They retired to their ivory towers, drew the curtains, and ignored the traffic outside. But habitual beliefs die hard, and for all their determination to live outside the sphere of public responsibility few of the Decadents were able to accept their position and rejoice wholeheartedly in their freedom. "The Dark Angel" and "Mystic and Cavalier" express Lionel Johnsons's dilemma most vividly; Richard Le Gallienne too, though the author of several Decadent poems and some privately circulated erotica, also wrote in praise of Platonic love, and denounced his contemporaries for their fondness of French lubricity; and Oscar Wilde, to give only one more example, described the rival attractions of the sphinx and the crucifix. Many of the Decadents were unequal to the struggle, and finding it impossible to reconcile the opposing forces which raged within, either gave up writing Decadent poetry altogether, died young, went mad, or entered the Church, but however the conflict ended, nearly all of them experienced with some pain the problems of reconciling the two sides of their nature. Ultimately, a split personality seems to characterize the late nineteenth-century Decadent more than any other quality.

It was the inability of the English Decadents to come

to terms with reality that most distressed Yeats. As he wrote in his *Autobiographies* (1926), they regarded poetry as "a terrible queen, in whose service the stars rose and set and for whose pleasure life stumbles along in the darkness." These poets looked upon art as a private pursuit wherein the sensitive person might escape from the vulgarity of the world, and find an outlet for his most personal revelations, or perhaps only for his artistic ingenuity. They refused to regard art as a means of understanding life. By contrast, a modern poet such as Wallace Stevens who, like the Decadents, was intensely preoccupied with architectonics, and who, also like the Decadents, owed a considerable debt to the Symbolist writers of France, regarded artistic creation as important because the artist is a symbol for man striving to "know," and thus the artistic product may be regarded as an interpretation of reality. Stevens accepted the validity of the poet's response, not simply for its own sake, but for the possibility of it being transformed into a symbol from which man might intuit something of the nature of the world in which he lives. There are, as Stevens noted, "thirteen ways of looking at a blackbird," but Victor Plarr in his poem "The Night Jar" could see only one, and that was conditioned by his Decadent predilections:

On the river, in the shallows, on the shore,
Are the darkness and the silence of the tomb;
O'er the woods the sunset dyed an hour before
    Utter gloom.

Only here betwixt the ramparts of tall trees,
In mid-stream, the pallid waters gleam afar,
Scarce a ripple on their surface, scarce a breeze,
    Scarce a star.

Where the shadow of the ruined water-mill

Hides the mill-pool and its anchored lily fleet,
And the warm air seems to slumber over-still,
  Over-sweet.

Hark the Night-jar! In the meadows by the stream
Shrills the bird's unearthly note: I like it well,
For it lulls you as the mystery of a dream,
  Or a spell.

All the nightingales along the bowery reach
Plain together when the midnight moon is bright:
This bird only knows the secret speech
  Of dark night.

Turn the boat now. Row away, friends. Let us hence,
Lest the glamour of the night's o'er-trancing breath,
Plunge us one and all into that dream intense
  Which is Death.

The inability of the Decadents to universalize their private emotions and transform them into generally significant experiences, has led most critics to disparage their verses. Certainly, judged by contemporary standards of artistic excellence there are few Decadent poems which deserve preservation from oblivion. Such pieces as Symons' "Japanese Dancers" and Dowson's "Cynara" have been consistently anthologized, and rightly so, but their merits are mainly technical. Nevertheless, Decadent poetry does have an important place in the history of the development of the English poetical tradition.

Most important, perhaps, the Decadents reaffirmed the primacy of individual feeling. They recognised the value of the private emotion, and were not afraid to seek their moments of rapture in a prostitute's arms or over a glass of absinthe. It is true that many of them seem to have felt that the only emotions worth having were to be found in the unsanctified areas of human experience, and it is also true that many of them give the impression that whether their experiences were significant or not, they were determined to make them so. Yet their example did free English verse from some of its moral inhibitions, and later poets were able to be less reticent in their choice of subject matter.

In matters of technique, too, the Decadents influenced the twentieth century. Too frequently it has been assumed that around 1900 there was a crisis, and somehow, within the space of a few years, there emerged a completely new kind of poetry which derived nothing from that of the previous century other than numerous examples of what was to be avoided. T. S. Eliot, Ezra Pound and T.E. Hulme all joined in denouncing what they regarded as the Romantic tradition, and resolved to set up new principles which would restore to English poetry those qualities which they felt had been lacking since the seventeenth century. Sentimentality and vagueness were to be avoided; the language was to reflect more closely the rhythms of everyday speech; and above all it was to demonstrate a "unification of sensibility." That is to say, the poem itself was to be a "non-discursive concetto" which would evoke rather than state the desired response. But for all the appearance this has of being revolutionary, as Frank Kermode has pointed out in his *Romantic Image*, such a theory is very similar to what the French Symbolists were proposing, to what Pater seems to have had in mind in his discussion of form and in his insistence on the aspiration of all art to a condition of music. Although there are few indications that the poets of the English Decadence were more than vaguely aware of the real significance of the masters they professed to follow, the fact that they did follow Pater and the French Symbolists surely makes it apparent that there was, after all, a definite link between the nineteenth century and the twentieth. At the very least, they did bring these writers clearly before the public eye, and though one may say that they worshipped them for wrong reasons, there were others who followed who recognised in them qualities which had escaped their predecessors. We should remember too that Arthur Symons was the man who first introduced Yeats, Eliot and Pound to French Symbolism, a debt which all of them freely acknowledged, and it was through his book, *The Symbolist Movement in Literature* (1899) that the aims and intentions of the Symbolist writers of France became known to English readers. It is true that apart from Frank Kermode and Ruth Temple, modern scholars have not treated Symons' efforts to unravel the complexities of the Symbolist aesthetic too kindly, and it cannot be denied that he oversimplifies the main issues. Yet, in the closing paragraph of his Introduction, he does adequately sum up the significance of this new literature, and point to those elements which have importance in the development of twentieth-century poetry:

> In this revolt against exteriority, against rhetoric, against a materialistic tradition; in this endeavor to disengage the ultimate essence, the soul, of whatever exists and can be realised by the consciousness; in this dutiful waiting upon every symbol by which the soul of things can be made visible; literature, bowed down by so many burdens, may at last attain liberty, and its authentic speech.

It would be too much to say that the English Decadent poets either aspired to or realised such aesthetic aims, yet many of them were obscurely aware of the issues involved, and in some of their poetry we can sense an uncertain groping towards such ideals. It is true that the twentieth century has found little to emulate in the characteristic poetry of the Decadent movement, but consciously or not it did find sufficient inspiration in the forces behind that poetry to develop an aesthetic appropriate to its needs, and it is primarily for this reason that the poetry of the English Decadence deserves more sympathetic attention than it has hitherto received.

Selected General Bibliography

Allen, Grant. "The New Hedonism," *Fortnightly Review*, LXI (1894), 377-392.

Archer, William. *Poets of the Younger Generation*, New York, 1902.

Beckson, Karl. *Aesthetes and Decadents of the 1890's: An Anthology of Prose and Verse*, New York, 1966.

Bowra, C.M. *The Heritage of Symbolism*, London, 1943.

Burdett, Osbert. *The Beardsley Period*, New York, 1925.

Buckley, Jerome H. *The Victorian Temper*, Cambridge, Mass., 1951.

Carter, A.E. *The Idea of Decadence in French Literature, 1830-1900*, Toronto, 1958.

Casford, E. Lenore. *The Magazines of the 1890's*, Eugene, Ore., 1929.

Charlesworth, Barbara. *Dark Passages: The Decadent Consciousness in Victorian Literature*, Madison, Wisc., 1965.

Chesterton, G.K. "Writing 'Finis' to Decadence," *Independent*, LXXXIX (1917), 100.

Dale, Hilda. *La Poésie Francaise en Angleterre: 1850-1890. Sa Fortune et son influence*, Paris, 1954.

Fletcher, Ian. "The 1890's: A Lost Decade," *Victorian Studies*, IV (1961), 345-354.

————. *Romantic Mythologies*, London, 1967.

Garbaty, Thomas Jay. "The French Coterie of *The Savoy* 1896," *PMLA*, LXXV (1960), 609-15.

Gaunt, William. *The Aesthetic Adventure*, New York, 1945.

Gerber, Helmut E. "The Nineties: Beginning, End, or Transition?" *Edwardians and Late Victorians*, ed. Richard Ellmann. New York, 1959.

Goldfarb, Russell M. "Late Victorian Decadence," *Journal of Aesthetics and Art Criticism*, XX (1962), 369-73.

Gosse, Edmund. *Modern English Literature*, New York, 1897.

Guérard, Albert. *Art for Art's Sake*, Boston, 1936.

Selected General Bibliography

Hamilton, W. *The Aesthetic Movement in England,* London, 1882.

Harris, Wendell. "Innocent Decadence: The Poetry of *The Savoy,*" *PMLA,* LXXVII (December, 1962), 629-36.

Hough, Graham. "George Moore and the Nineties," *Edwardians and Late Victorians,* ed. Richard Ellmann, New York, 1959.

————. *The Last Romantics.* London, 1949.

Hunt, John Dixon. *The Pre-Raphaelite Imagination 1848-1900,* London, 1968.

Jackson, Holbrook. *The Eighteen Nineties,* New York, 1913.

Jepson, Edgar. *Memories of a Victorian,* London, 1933.

Kermode, Frank. *Romantic Image,* New York, 1957.

Le Gallienne, Richard. *The Romantic 90's,* New York, 1925.

————, "What's Wrong with the Eighteen-Nineties," *The Bookman,* LIV (1921), 1-7.

Lehmann, A.G. *The Symbolist Aesthetic in France, 1885-1895,* Oxford, 1950.

May, J. Lewis. *John Lane and the Nineties,* London, 1936.

Mix, Katherine. *A Study in Yellow: The Yellow Book and Its Contributors,* Lawrence, Kansas, 1960.

Moers, Ellen. *The Dandy: Brummel to Beerbohm,* New York, 1960.

Moore, George. *Confessions of a Young Man,* London, 1916.

Muddiman, Bernard. *The Men of the Nineties,* London, 1920.

Murdoch, G. Blaikie. *The Renaissance of the Nineties,* London, 1911.

Peters, Robert L. "Towards an 'Un-Definition' of Decadent as Applied to British Literature of the Nineteenth Century," *Journal of Aesthetics and Art Criticism,* XVIII (December, 1959), 258-64.

————. "Whistler and the English Poets of the 1890's," *Modern Language Quarterly,* XVIII (September, 1957), 251-61.

Pick, John. "Divergent Disciples of Walter Pater," *Thought,* XXIII (1948), 114-128.

Praz, Mario. *The Romantic Agony,* London, 1933.

Priestley, J.B. (ed.). *The Book of Bodley Head Verse,* London, 1926.

Quilter, Harry. "The Gospel of Intensity," *Macmillan's Magazine,* XLII (1880), 391-400.

————. "The Gospel of Intensity," *Macmillan's Magazine,* XLIII (1880), 80.

—————. "The Gospel of Intensity," *Contemporary Review*, LXVII (1895), 761-782.

Rhys, Ernest. *Everyman Remembers*, London, 1931.

—————. *Letters From Limbo*, London, 1936.

Richards, Grant. *Memories of a Misspent Youth*, New York, 1933.

Robinson, James K. "A Neglected Phase of the Aesthetic Movement: English Parnassianism," *PMLA*, LXVIII (1953), 733-54.

Rosenblat Louise. *L'Idée de l'art pour l'art dans la littérature anglaise pendant la période victorienne*, Paris, 1931.

Rossetti, William M. "The Gospel of Intensity," *Macmillian's Magazine*, XLIII (1880), 80.

Rothenstein, Sir William. *Men and Memories* (2 vols.), London, 1931.

Ryals, Clyde de L. "The Nineteenth-Century Cult of Inaction," *Tennessee Studies in Literature*, IV (1959), 51-60.

—————. "Towards a Definition of Decadent as Applied to British Literature of the Nineteenth Century," *Journal of Aesthetics and Art Criticism*, XVII (September 1958), 85-92.

Schaffer, Aaron. *Parnassus in France*, Austin, Texas, 1929.

Secker, Martin. ed. *The Eighteen-Nineties. A Period Anthology in Prose and Verse*, with an introduction by John Betjeman, London, 1948.

Starkie, Enid. *From Gautier to Eliot: The Influence of France on English Literature, 1851-1939*, London, 1960.

Stutfield, Hugh E.M. "Tommyrotics," *Blackwood's Magazine*, CLVII (1895), 833-845.

Symons, A.J.A. (ed.). *An Anthology of 'Nineties Verse*, London, 1928.

Temple, Ruth Z. *The Critic's Alchemy: A Study of the Introduction of Symbolism into England*, New York, 1953.

—————. "The Ivory Tower as Lighthouse," *Edwardians and Late Victorians*, ed. Richard Ellmann, New York, 1959.

Weintraub, Stanley, ed. *The Savoy: Nineties Experiment*, University Park, Pa., 1965.

—————. *The Yellow Book: Quintessence of the Nineties*, Garden City, New York, 1966.

West, Paul. "A Note on the 1890's," *English* XII (1958), 54-57.

Wilcox, John. "The Beginnings of L'Art pour L'Art," *Journal of Aesthetics and Art Criticism*, XI (June, 1953), 360-77.

Selected General Bibliography

William, Harold. *Outlines of Modern English Literature: 1890-1914*, New York, 1920.

Winwar, Frances. *Oscar Wilde and the Yellow 'Nineties*, New York, 1940.

Wright, Cuthbert. "Out of Harm's Way: Some Notes on the Esthetic Movement of the 'Nineties," *The Bookman*, LXX (1929), 234-438.